MY ROBERTO CLEMENTE

RICK HILLES

C&R Press
Conscious & Responsible

Winter Soup Bowl Selection
2021 7th Collection Selection 2 of 2 CB 14

All Rights Reserved

Printed in the United States of America

First Edition
1 2 3 4 5 6 7 8 9

Selections of up to two pages may be reproduced without permissions. To reproduce more than two pages of any one portion of this book write to C&R Press publishers John Gosslee and Andrew Ibis.

Cover Art and Cover by Anna Magruder

Copyright ©2021 Rick Hilles

ISBN 978-1-949540-28-4

C&R Press
Conscious & Responsible
crpress.org
Long Live Books!

For discounted bulk purchases, and other items please contact C&R Press sales@crpress.org

MY ROBERTO CLEMENTE

Contents

My Roberto Clemente   7

Mission Statement   9

To the Language Spoken in the Country of Urgency   11

Song for the Vultures   12

Sex after Fifty   13

For the Wall-Sized Murals Marc Chagall Painted for the Moscow Yiddish Theater   14

My Polish   16

Another Poem that I Can't Show to My Sweetheart's Parents   18

Semaj   21

Seven for the Last Words of X   23

    "X, which marks a spot for the unknown..."   23

    "One day, the ships on the horizon..."   24

    "In this version of our story..."   25

    "Here lies the mother's son: see..."   26

    "Here, the point of wolves is a yellow fang, the bright edge..."   27

    "No one knew her heart had not grown properly..."   28

    "If only each of us, as we are constructed now..."   39

Of Ancient Music & the Perceivable Spectrum   30

The Perplexities of Time & Space at Last Explained (Eventually, Despite Rain Delays)   32

Accidental Reunion with My Kid Sister on Our Father's 79th Birthday   34

For the Beater Car That Managed to Give Us a Forced Vacation in the Poconos on my Birthday   36

The Flying Carpet   40

In the Book of Spells   42

To Misunderstanding   43

Family Secrets   44

The Invisible Thread   46

My Brother, The Poet, at Nineteen   54
Sightings   55
"City Ducks"   56

Acknowledgments 58

For You

MY ROBERTO CLEMENTE

Doesn't everyone need a charm—like a lucky rabbit's foot?—
    but something with the power to transform,
even mutate in ways that might save us, especially when
        all the rules have changed?

    In those first board games of childhood
when "house rules" so often meant the power to change
the rules at the house's whim, you needed your own hand-
    sized "Get out of jail free!" jet-pack of transformation.

You needed a Roberto Clemente. Your own ace-in-the-hole.

As a kid, I laid down my best baseball cards when I saw my friend
    put up for grabs his Roberto Clemente, the Puerto Rican
Willie Mays, who was so devoted to the people of his homelands
        that he died delivering them earthquake relief.

    And now that children again are donning
adult clothes, how to prevent them from running
roughshod over us but by devising our own emergency trump cards?
    But how to take this metaphor to the next level?

What's your Roberto Clemente? What's your ace-in-the-hole?

What's one thing no one can take from you? One thing not
    even hit-men can destroy? Sure, they can lace you
with nerve agents and bone-saw you all the way from
        the Red Sea to the Bosphorus.

    But once you say your piece and make peace
with it, neither can be undone. You might ask, But what if
I'm not around to play my Roberto Clemente? My ace-in-the-hole?
    The words keep doing what you've taught them to do.

The Puerto Rican Willie Mays keeps hitting another home run
"Through the entire Anglo-Saxon tradition," as Ferlinghetti said.
Nevermind they never found his body in the wreckage
of the DC-7 he insisted on riding, so one more plane delivering

relief to Managua would not be diverted by one more corrupt politician.
(As were the first three planes!) What mattered to Clemente
was that the resources got to where they needed to go. That's why
we remember him—and forget the rest.

So what's your Roberto Clemente? What's your ace-in-the-hole?

MISSION STATEMENT

I want to design an amusement park
that doesn't make me want to throw up.
I want to invent a board game
that rewards each player
for solving the problems of the world,
that takes points off for
gratuitous acts of pure unkindness
and for each move of mere advantage
over others, which is how we got here
in the first place; I want to devise
a pastime to harness the energy
of all the squandered hours
between us, of all the nights and days
stacked end to end of when we wished
to kill time before we thought better
of how to deploy it for curing the world's ills
that plague us even now threatening
to wipe out every species and saving us for last;
I want to manufacture a unit of currency
as plentiful as the shade and as
unpocketable and as deaf to greed,
avarice and false counsel as some
haircuts are completely impervious
to passing fads and market trends.
I want to promote a manner of affection
bereft of affectation, though it may
occasionally involve a squirt-gun bow-tie.
I want to arrive at the right theorem
to account for all the errors
in judgment that have landed us
in the prison of our current dilemma,
an equal and opposite compensatory action
to counteract every offending gesture.
It will require so much more
than me or any one life can rightfully achieve

but maybe if enough of us sign on to it
there's no telling what we can do
to elude the impending catastrophe.

TO THE LANGUAGE SPOKEN IN THE COUNTRY OF URGENCY

"In the country of urgency, there is a language."
—Grace Schulman

I must have said something
to the man in my confusion

when I put my hand on his
shoulder long enough for

a cement truck to breeze by
—it would have killed him—

instantly, I think, when the light
changes and its change falls

through our long shadows,
spreading the news of sunset

over our faces and the wet streets
and we—the temporary single

organism of crowd—begin again
to cross the street, when the man

turns to face me now and asks
if I know Arabic. (I say, I wish!)

"Because just then it sounded
a lot like you were calling me

by name in the language of
my other mother country!"

SONG FOR THE VULTURES

Go ahead, call us Bottom Feeders, Death's
                Opportunists, Shadows Circling
        the Toilet Bowl. But now Overhead.
And Blotting Out the Sun. To see us, first
                you must crane your necks

and squint—to know somebody's done for.
                When will it be you, you wonder?
        Not now, not tomorrow. Not even the next day.
Or the next. But much sooner than you think, I fear.
                There are ways, though, for you to know

when we are finally onto you: a weakness
                that pulls you to the ground.
        A metallic taste that no food or drink softens.
Your awareness of us on your scent, in your periphery
                entering your orbit. Would you ever be

so brave as the Tibetans who leave their remains for us
                knowing how we will jockey for position
        to pluck out especially the delicate eyeballs!—
that we might have our own human visions of the setting sun?
                Though you may always fear

the way we appear so suddenly as sharks, our wingspans
                that unnerve you as you watch us
        descending on another creature that refuses
to admit that it is now little more than road kill. Carrion.
                Know this, that we will come for you

one day, but not a moment before we are ready to reclaim
                you on behalf of the living—
        for what once nourished you now nourishes us.
Until we too are awakened by the same metallic taste.
                And we know at last our day is done.

SEX AFTER FIFTY
*—for a friend who, on his fiftieth birthday, received a book
with this title as a gift which, when opened,
revealed that all the pages were completely blank*

It's a lot better than you might think, especially
if the thought of it makes you a little queasy.
For one thing, your looks are just starting
to get interesting—and everything else
that's starting to sag, wilt, or whatever
was never really what it was all about
in the first place. While it may be nice to dream
that you will just lean into the splendor
of sensations in total darkness, most times
it's better to leave a light on and reflect
on how much more comfortable you are
in your skin. (Not to mention, somebody else's!)
So, while you're still holding the universe
in place on its axis, the two of you now
pinned to each other and your shadows, holding
everything, including even the outmoded notions
that could use a little more entertaining these days
like the Music of the Spheres, which will sing
its immortal shape into you a little more each time
you come to know love in rapturous sex after fifty!

FOR THE WALL-SIZED MURALS MARC CHAGALL PAINTED FOR THE MOSCOW YIDDISH THEATER
—hidden during WWII and brought safely out of hiding in a ceremony with the artist fifty years after Chagall completed them

He painted them in his twenties. And yet
everything we love about him is already here.
Even several things I'd forgotten, including
how he can keep your eyes focused on a dancer

leaping in the middle of a canvas, and only
when your eyes settle, do you see another man
—part Talmudic scholar, part sideshow freak—
relieving himself on a circus tent with such ecstasy.

On another, an almost beatifically-joyous man
has his pants down, squatting beside an outhouse.
As if to remind us how close they always hover,
the sacred and profane. So palpable both are here

you begin to wonder: What other aspects of life
would have died had Chagall not captured them?
Even what was erased beyond all recognition
still shimmers in the colors of the floating clarinetist

as he blows a rainbow fountain into the night air
in which he levitates. It feels good to be reminded,
too, of the Talmudic principle enacted in these
canvases—that saving one life saves the entire world—

and I thought I saw around these figures painted
so rapidly—the air around insects preserved in amber.
That each canvas contained its own miniature city
that stirs in us (if shaken) a night of fresh falling snow.

I want to hold all these images in my astonishment
and to be an extension of the preserving element

that holds each living thing at its moment of extinction
to preserve the radiance still alive inside our world.

MY POLISH

When I try to thank it, it shushes me. Then illuminates my way to the Exit.
What little Polish I have
likes me best when I'm trying harder to deserve it. Meanwhile, it will have
none of my shenanigans.

Least of all my pocket phrasebook sayings. Even if those who have spoken
her their whole lives sometimes
encourage me with an "Oh, your Polish is so good!" when I simply say Hi!
on a train, what little Polish I have

knows better, and elbows me in the ribs, then she just laughs and laughs.
Lately, she seems to prefer me
when I am at a perfect loss with her and have to ask her all kinds of questions.
Then, she looks me in the eye

and seems to take a genuine interest. I fear, though, that I remain too eager
for her ever to give me the key
to her innermost rooms, so I might bask in her albums of Chopin and come
to comprehend her great depths

and secrets. Clearly she reserves these intimacies for others who've earned her
    trust, her almost family, who have
proven their fidelity to her over many years. If not decades. Even then, sometimes
    she needs more proof of loyalty.

To hear them say a shibboleth I never had. Even without her password, still I
    pursue her sometimes like a lover
who sees his having a beautiful future with her. I have to admit. It is unlikely.
    Yet sometimes even now that

kind of seeing, and love, well up in me. I'm inclined to think my Polish—
    promiscuous as she is—
encourages it. How else could she have survived those generations of occupation
    and partition? But for the many mouths

that coveted her cigarette and pastry taste. Even now, the sudden whiff of wild
    mushrooms. Maybe in an autumn broth.
Or a particularly gamey sausage will bring her back, the way a smile on the Sphinx
    still trembles with the riddle of her Great Mysteries.

ANOTHER POEM THAT I CAN'T SHOW TO MY SWEETHEART'S PARENTS

for Walter and Marie

Of course I have to dedicate this poem to my sweetheart's parents
even if they are likely never to read it.
Which reminds me just a little bit of the fun fact I heard on NPR once about
crickets—who make noises that we can hear
but at a frequency that never reaches their own ears.
(If they can be said to have ears!)

Which makes me wonder if there is a music that we can make
that others can receive, even if it never reaches our own ears?
So maybe this also means that there is also a music we make that we can hear
even if certain others never get to hear it?
The writers behind the Iron (or was it Velvet?) Curtain had something like this
in their mimeographed Samizdat editions:

Those years that Ivan Klima and Zbigniew Herbert
were thought to write only for the top drawers of their desks
publishing nothing in the nationally approved presses and passing their poems
and stories along to friends—in copies of purple-blue ink.

But please don't think, Walter and Marie, that I'm trying to leave you
out with the freezing rain and decaying leaves,

equating you it seems with the Communist censors who were so disapproving
of free thought and individual expression that they accused
poets like Joseph Brodsky of being "parasites of the State." It is the far
more insidious relation between intolerance and ideology
that makes me link totalitarian regimes, even and especially those
founded on Marx's premise

that "Religion is the opiate of the masses!" with religious fundamentalism.
I imagine you'll be offended by this analogy, and forgive me if
it does offend, but the poet's work, at least as I understand it, is to make
such connections, even and especially where these
conjoinings of twins make us most uncomfortable, even writhing
a little with the clarities

that they give rise to in us—the more we sit with them. But now I feel
the need to return to an analogy I made earlier, or, really, more
of a question that I asked: Is there a music that we can make that is only
for others and not our own ears? If there is, how would
we ever know there is? Unless others heard it and told us
what it means to them.

19

As part of me—a surprising to me large part of me—wishes, really hopes
that either or both of you will find a way to communicate with
your daughter and me to tell us that some music that we're somehow
responsible for, but have no knowledge of directly,
has found its way to you and you have been glad to bask in it.
And maybe while it doesn't

jive completely with your fundamentalist Christian beliefs, somehow
it still speaks to you nevertheless, and kisses you with its beauty.
Maybe you are hardly even aware of hearing it, let alone what it says,
but one morning you wake with an almost unspeakable
tenderness filling your eyes, your whole body lit with some dawning
recognition you want to call, Holy.

And even as you have this immense sense of opening, all day,
it's still too much to speak about to anyone. And yet, somehow,
this same music fills even the awkward silences between us.
And nourishes you both, and all of us, even when
we're not listening. Oh, Walter and Marie! If you were to ask me
sometime what all of that is

I'd tell you both: To me, that's poetry!

SEMAJ

Oh, thank you, Semaj, for smiling at me and saying Hello!
        at the annual Symphony Space sidewalk book sale,
    your four-year-old-boy self already up to my waist.
        By now you will have forgotten me
as you're supposed to, so you can have room in your still-forming brain
    for all the things you really need to learn, including

your multiplication tables, the Declaration of Independence,
        the capitals to the states and nations of the world.
    I'll consider it an honor when you replace your memory of me
        with the Heimlich maneuver, or something
that could help you in an emergency—as valuable as 9-1-1—
    anything to help you save a life, especially your own.

But I don't need to forget about you so easily. For one thing,
    I'm at an age when forgetting things
comes too easily, and remembering is an act of resistance.
        And I aim to resist the dying of my light.
And so what, if others deem this moment worthy of forgetting?
    I shall preserve you, if only in the amber of this memory.

I can still see you turning to me when you said, "Rick, look!" and
        your impish dimples sparkled as the books you stacked
    made the most perfect launching pad for your water bottle.
        (One third full as its contents sloshed
inside, not ruining a single book, which clearly delighted you!)
    So, you're a builder, are you? I asked. And you said, Yes!

I am a builder! Your four-year-old self and your mother just in
        Manhattan for the day, taking the train in from the Bronx.
    And even if I remember your first name now forever
        as your mother laughingly explained it to me:
"Semaj! It's James backwards!"—nothing will ever diminish
    the meaning you gave your name today all by yourself.

A meaning inseparable now, at least in my mind, from that book
            of Nelson Mandela's favorite children's stories
    at Symphony Space. Which your mother let me buy for you,
            your smile by now so ginormous
it seemed you'd eaten the whole big apple and the sun in that instant
        when I gave you the book, as if returning it to its rightful owner.

SEVEN FOR THE LAST WORDS OF X

—written for a performance of Haydn, based on the last seven utterances of Christ, and written in the wake of the shootings of Trayvon Martin, Jordan Davis, Renisha McBride and now so many others.

1.

X, which marks a spot for the unknown,
X, for the variable we can't solve,
the treasure just below our feet, X,
for those we don't know who, nevertheless,
give all that we may persist—X, for what
lies under every flame—X, for the martyr's
charred fallen cross, for the one who said
of his tormentors: "Forgive them, for they
know not what they do!" X, for the kiss
that singes our flesh, even now, X, for each
name that does not fit—some brutal legacy,
a final violence of master to slave, as for
Malcolm, or the way a mother's right to
sign her work—which we *all* are—in one
gesture is erased. And so an X, to honor
these on whom we stand, we, drawn from
the living soil (which knows no single oath
or fealty but that of our shared betterment).
X marks the spot, for what lies buried in us,
still waiting to be unearthed, and may be yet,
so long as we listen—X, for the clear instant
that insists on our presence for the story to
begin, as it must, and grow in the attention of
others, in whom we live, long after our story ends.

2.

One day, the ships on the horizon,
clinging like insects to the wet rind
of the world, will enlarge and come
for you, to take you past the island
of yourself, toward the distant music
that only now you begin to hear—
the sounds of a far-off place, wind-
swept, imagined, if by imagined
we mean unreal, and so alive with all
we do not know—and will not know,
ever—before the music summons us
there; where we may come to say
to those who deliver us: "The longer
I live, the less sure I am of what I know!"
So that when you are summoned,
hearing: "Today you will join me
in Paradise," the words stop you
in your tracks, no matter how much
the breeze rushing through you with
its clarifying air broadens your sails.

3.

In this version of our story, Death
passes over us, again, and we are spared,
if only once before that distant music
summons us, bending our final attention
to its will. Say that, if you were spared,
Death would take another in your place.
In the thrall of that last awakening,
what would you do? If Death, looking
to meet its daily quota of souls, seized the lost
shade of a boy, the latest lost to violence?

Mother, Behold Thy Son,
                              the coroner says
without a sound but for the slide of
morgue drawer, out and in.
                              Another X,
—now, for another you will never know—
whose loss you will observe each time
a floorboard creaks under your feet.

4.

Here lies the mother's son: see how
the bones articulate the flesh, the way
that light unfolds, each crease, each
fold and contour, wherever sensation,
idea, thought, insight once moved—
sometimes a fleeing eel, a nervous squirrel,
or a series of clouds filling the mind, angry
storms, a green wind gathering in bare limbs.
Here is the place where the pages of
the day's intrigues turn to our worst fears,
where love and grief, reverie and pain would
surface like a manatee drawn instinctively
to the warmer regions between worlds.

> *"My God, My God! – Why have you forsaken me?"*

The man's mother says, or seems to say,
her whole body convulsing in a green light.

And the promise of the son, what woke
in him—nightly, daily, in the living cells—
vanishes—the snail and all its meat,
retreating to the farthest reaches of its shell.

5. (Point Lobos)

Here, the point of wolves is a yellow fang, the bright edge of the world. Above the wild Pacific, the earth sun-scorched to glassy sand, thirsting.

Below, the Cliff House, Seal Rocks, where for a decade, no sea lions (the "seals") sunned themselves after Loma Prieta (the Quake of '89).

Then, the cusp of the millennium, El Niño boiled, forcing sardine, mackerel, and white sea bass North. Sea lions chased them all to these white stained rocks and again lay claim to them.

                                                Other places change.
In Central Michigan, a confirmed sighting of a wolverine—the first in two centuries.
            East, in the Adirondacks, warming weather now brings mountain lions from Canada back to the U.S. each Spring.

Advice, if confronted by a mountain lion:
                        "APPEAR LARGER THAN YOU ARE."

When I rounded the corner junco shrub on a dusty hillcrest road in northern California's Santa Cruz Mountains, I saw a swaggering muscular silhouette of a full-grown cougar cross my path and pivot, turning all its power on me, its ropy heavy-weight boxer's shoulders rippling down to whip-crack of tail. I looked it in the eye and slowly backed away.
            If you love your life at all, don't look away. Face what can kill you. (Soon enough, a silhouette appears.) Stare it down. Look it in the eye: Directly. Then, for the sake of everything you will ever love, slowly—*slowly!*—back away.

6.

No one knew her heart had not grown properly.
Tiny arteries, tiny veins. Failing her at fifty.
Her doctor says six months. Surgery? Risky.

Worth a try. She has to be kept awake.
In the surgical theater, she hears everything.
Imagine. One surgeon gives up. "I am done!"

"That's it for me," she thinks. Will we all think
this? How many face death without kindness?
(Could she feel what was beyond the room?)

The surgeon calls for a replacement. A guy
who looks thirteen appears. He says: "Okay.
Listen up. We're going to *do* this. Together

we'll rebuild this woman's heart!" The woman
can almost feel the man-boy's squirrely hands
thread the red and blue wires to her damaged

arteries and veins. Hours pass. She hears
orchestral sounds. Then voices: Children singing.
"I must be dead," she thinks. "It is finished."

The surgery is complete. But outside
the O.R., real children are singing. Two long-
haired girls and a woman, their mother, hold

signs for the man-boy surgeon. *Happy Birthday,
Daddy!* Then they embrace the wiry, geek-
squad guy (still weaving like a boxer). Beneath

his curly, red shock of hair, he grins his wise-
ass sweetheart grin. It's his birthday. He's saved
our friend. Eight years later, she's teaching again.

Living up north with her own sweetheart.

7.

If only each of us, as we are constructed now—
of flesh, desire, will and bone—
were led back to that waterfall
where light collides with rising mist
our faces damp with gratitude
at our return, in late Summer, to see and breathe
and taste again the scents of early Spring
as they blaze new trails and pathways
in the mind—bright filaments, flickering
neurons, the flash of heat lightning—
in which we see ourselves beyond ourselves.
The secret sense of flowers saturates the air,
an atmosphere that carries us as we carry it,
even here. A distant music summons us
again to that first wonder, of water rising
in air, of the light that opens us
to ways deserving of ourselves and of the earth—
and to you—whom I invoke, without
acquaintance, yet hope to do well by, all the same.
To tend to what is yours as much as ours.
For this I stand and commit myself: To you.

OF ANCIENT MUSIC & THE PERCEIVABLE SPECTRUM

In the book of unbelievable facts
                called Unbelievable Facts
    (the "Indisputable Collection" of "True-Life Facts")
        you can read of how the sand swept
up in desert winds blasted the faces of figures
    that adorned, often sitting before, the Great Pyramids.
          One funeral temple near Thebes

built by Amenhotep III in the 15th century B.C.E.
                had two "colossal stone statues"
    that sat on either side of the road leading to the great temple
        guarding its entrance. In the centuries
that followed their miraculous construction, the book says
    that worshippers nearing the temple at sunrise or sunset
            (by camel or by foot) heard the strangest sounds

emanating from these figures. The Ancient Greeks described
                the noises—harrowing in their own right—
as being harp-like, a kind of hand-plucked tidal resonance
        from these massive, near sixty-foot tall, figures.
They resumed at the same time every morning, sounds like wind
    raking through the pipes of a church organ, but in shapes
        that sang for everyone who approached them

until an earthquake disfigured the twins, the Colossi of Memnon.
        It was only when Roman Emperor
Septimus Severus demanded that the figures be restored
        to their prior splendor that they were repaired.
Though the figures were never heard singing again. Whether
    one way of knowing had eclipsed another way of knowing
        or that somehow the nasal-like passageways

in the statuary had caved in or something else—no one knows.
Today, the great temple of Amenhotep the III
is eroded completely, though the Colossi of Memnon remain—
still guarding what they were erected to protect
(treasures no longer visible to the naked eye) with their colossal strength.
In the last few years, though, visitors of the ruins say that
the figures are making their unreal sounds again.

No one knows what treasures the Colossi of Memnon guard to this day,
which are buried so deep and far
from our view, or if the priceless heist of their pharaoh still exists.
But another theory for the sound the statues make maintains
that the singing is meant to protect those who come to perceive it.
So, if you hear the sound—the sound now welling up in you—
you will not give in to temptation. Doubt.

Or second thought. And the music preserving you will continue
as on a harp, breathing on your heart-strings,
and you will understand that you're what's at risk of being squandered
at any moment and you will promise, to the music
singing inside you now, that you have not come this far—to the shadows
of the Great Pyramids—to waste your energies on useless things.
And you will hear the singing inside you again

the next time you need to be set free.

THE PERPLEXITIES OF TIME & SPACE AT LAST EXPLAINED (EVENTUALLY, DESPITE RAIN DELAYS)

—for Lucie Brock-Broido

I've cashed in my Cathedral-quiet for a few well-worn African drums.

And a Sengalese Punic mask that I was gifted, I believe, by Oblivion.

After talking with a magical friend over an ordinary dinner one night

Then walking home alone in the bustle of mid-summer urban darkness

I heard the sound of something
                                  Had it been thrown from a passing car?

Or fallen from a great height?
                            Who can say? But picking it up, I saw

A hand-carved face
                of an African woman, at rest, the skin painted

A ghostly white
                the black carvings of her hair
                                        an image that I'd learn
Only later
        is meant to bring its bearer   to the end   of grief

Now that I have enjoyed its companionable silence for a whole year

I give it to you now
                    That you might know its living medicine

Like a blank page
                preparing for the soul that will seek refuge on it

May you receive

               its bounty   inexhaustible   as it is delicious

You, with your husky lounge-singer voice tongue-tied from twirling

Cherry-stems   into gift bows

                                  With your immaculate tobacco mouth

ACCIDENTAL REUNION WITH MY KID SISTER ON OUR FATHER'S SEVENTY-NINTH BIRTHDAY

       A quiet evening derailed by emergency (benign):
my sister's connecting flight from Glasgow to Chicago
          via Newark is canceled due to heavy rain,
     rain that my love and I, only hours before, were
kicking back into the teeth of the yellow cabs that splashed us
          in our improvised garbage bag raincoats.

       You can tell a lot about yourself by how you
respond in such moments. How I knew why my sister was calling
          before she said a word. And I didn't
     even pause at all when she added, "…Oh, and
my friend, too!" But I didn't know at all what she meant exactly when
          she said she was "transitioning," it meaning

       now, well, so many things. Was she "coming out"
to me now in some way? And was I the first (or already last?)
          to know? "…Vaping, I don't smoke
     cigarettes anymore! Apparently, the research
says it's less harmful." And you really want to encourage your kid sister
          especially in her attempts to elude

       a predatory industry. (Even if, by now, we know that vaping
has its problems, too.) For now, all you know is that these two women
          who you in your benign oldster way call "kids"
     won't eat if you don't serve them, so you father them
with cherries right from the fridge, good cheese, dried mangoes, papaya,
          and they daughter you, happy to regale you in stories

    mostly of delayed luggage and boys. Your sister's friend
may need to stay after your sister leaves—a day or two, maybe more—
      and to that you also say Okay, encouraging them
    not to think of it, or of their chances to book better flights,
before they've had a chance to sleep, and they're too tired not to agree.
      Other years, you might have felt guilty

    for having lost all that time when you could have been
working. Now you know if not better, then that to be a comfort to anyone
       in the shit-storm of the world, and on your father's birthday,
    is the calling of the angels in whom you don't even believe—
though you are happy to do their bidding, especially for your sister
      and her friend, and so you do, and you're glad to be alive.

FOR THE BEATER CAR THAT MANAGED
TO GIVE US A FORCED VACATION IN THE
POCONOS ON MY FIFTY-THIRD BIRTHDAY

Oh, second-hand Honda Civic EX, I thank you!
And I thank your first owner, my friend and former colleague, Jaya Kasibhatla,
a specialist in Post-Colonial Theory
who ditched the tenure-track for NYU law
and now lives with her husband and infant son in Park Slope,
so ferociously brilliant

and ingenious that maybe only she could have commanded
such a miraculous performance out of you, or, in this case, the timeliness
of your malfunction: my birthday.
This year, the Sunday after Thanksgiving,
your defrost so overtaxed by freezing rains on our drive in from
Cleveland to Manhattan

to see a friend's play, a thought-child we'd met
in its gestation period all of two years before. It's something to celebrate:
The first steps of any imaginary
offspring, especially for us, the "thought-birthers"

whose children, all unreal, still cast real shadows on real walls.
          After the after-party, driving
     our playwright friend Frank back to his home in Jersey
in the worst freezing rain I've ever driven in, that daggery, apocalyptic downpour
                    nearly did us in, were it not for you!
          After breakfast with Frank and Hen, the clearest skies
above New Jersey, pure robin's eggshell blue, the clouds just arriving,
               we left with full bellies and hearts

          for our next road trip adventure, driving not even an hour
before that unmistakable engine sound, as if machinery were capable of mocking
               Harvey Fierstein, his torchlit drag queen voice,
          but where you least want to hear it: in your engine.
We were still in New Jersey when we pulled off the highway,
               the toll booth worker kindly directing us

     to the nearest garage. Before long, the hood's up,
and both of us are on our Iphones, surrounded by the most beautiful, if dilapidated
               Victorian homes I'd ever dreamt of owning,
          when a stranger approached, more like a thirty-something
hipster or a surgeon than mass-murderer, who asked me once to rev the motor
                    and instantly diagnosed the problem

telling us which local garage to take you to, and more
immediately pressing for us both now, where best to spend the night.
We thanked him with such intensity
that he disappeared, like a drummer from Spinal Tap.
(I'm sure he didn't really spontaneously combust!) And we were having a forced vacation
in the Poconos, thanks to you. I never
suspected anything, until Anna and I found ourselves
inside the mountain town's old factory's blackened red brick walls: now
a wall to wall flea market with knick-knacks
where we found an abundance of discarded antiques
we didn't need, when we happened on one then two
folk art curiosities our lives were better having:
one, a blue bird carved out of driftwood and whimsy;
the other, a red fish hammered from rusty metal and painted in alternating
red and white stripes, as if made by rogue cartoonists
who, in an unauthorized experimental short, depicted
Wile E. Coyote at last catching the elusive Road Runner, as Anna and I
caught these most elusive gifts of time and space.

Thanks to you! And, so, I write this note of gratitude
to you, so that if and when you read this, Dear Jaya, you will know
why I've yet to part with your old car.
It's not just because you sold it to me for a song,
one that keeps on singing, however off-key; as Jeremy
my go-to guy at the Honda Dealership
says, "Most Civics are just finding themselves at 200,000 miles!"
And though the ceiling upholstery peeled off long ago, the visors
torn to shreds from when you, Jaya,
baby-sat those rescue cats, I still see no point
in replacing a working car, in an age when everything is made
to fall apart, so I'll hold onto you, dependable
friend, for as long as can, and only ask that you not be
insulted when I finally trade you in, or sell you, as I did my last Honda
twenty years ago: to a grad student in Psychology
at U of M; though I no longer recall his name
he sent me a road-trip photo of himself with that blue Honda Civic
on a red butte in Arizona, so I promise I won't
sell you, until I find a prospective owner as deserving as him!

THE FLYING CARPET

It hovered just above the surface of the earth, the carpet
                that moved like an unearthed piece of sidewalk
    an inch above the sidewalk, the shadow sidewalk moving
                        but made up entirely of ants
        a shadowy rectangular cauldron moving, moving,

moving now almost impossibly up the stairs toward him
            in the small Guatemalan village
    where he lived that summer, where scorpions
                      seemed to find you everywhere.
      Appearing sometimes only when you'd forgotten them

crawling into view from the undersides of, say,
            kitchen tables. His hammock kept him
    safe, unless he saw one on the ceiling. Or stepped on one.
                    Once he found a deadly one
    on a loose roll of toilet paper he'd grabbed

without looking first, a mistake he'd never make again. So, he was
            always trip-wire taut now and ready to snap
    when he caught sight of the carpet of ants ascending the fieldstone steps
                    hugging the edges without stopping
    in the midday heat, which could play with your mind

anyway, and leave you like an exposed nerve, even when you've slept.
            They were just beyond his lengthening shadow when
    he leapt to his feet, grabbed the bucket of last night's rain water,
                      and threw it on the teeming army of ants
        making them scatter at once into the lush, tall grass.

That night he met some friends for drinks and told them all about
            his encounter with the low flying carpet of ants
    and how he'd dispatched them with a pail of water when one local said
                  "The carpet of ants! That's about
    the only thing that will rid your house of scorpions!"

Then the man said, just earlier that season, he'd seen one of
        the deadliest scorpions taken down by such an overflowing
swarm. He said it was like watching a great castle sink into the sea,
                its despot still in the ramparts, surveying
the wreckage, as the assailing generations bring him down.

IN THE BOOK OF SPELLS

In the book of old spells—some promising
to bring rain while others assure safe passage
for our dead, from here to whatever's next—
I search for words that might help us now,
past curses that for others are the cures.
Turning the pages makes a crisp, bright sound.
There's something in moving through this
book alone that comforts as it gives gooseflesh.
So much power in one carefully constructed
tome, and yet each recipe for transformation
stares back silent as a gargoyle on a tomb.
Even if I could cast a spell, what would I invoke?
(The cure might be far worse than the curse!)
Maybe this book is too powerful for anyone
to own? (The press was small and now is defunct.)
Like those who see the holy words of sacred texts
transcribed on what they eat, now I see more
in each seed that might be planted in the earth.
Maybe the ancients saved their best magic
not for words but for what comes to us when
we are overtaken by the sight of a loved one
and words fail us, or we fail them, when we
are wrong in how we're being right, and truth
eludes us. And now I read of how some wishes
were bound with twine (or hair—one's own
or of a lover, living or dead) and tied to stones
which were thrown to various bodies of water,
where they traveled the current that carried
them, and dissolved. Already, the book says,
by now, we've washed ourselves so many times
in all the waters holding the ancients wishes
that the answers they sought still hover near us.
Finally, I close the forbidden book and rise
so I can stand where the answers already are.

TO MISUNDERSTANDING

On the radio today, a neurologist identified
the most important capacity
of the human brain
as being its capacity to contemplate
a self beyond itself. Even the interviewer was not so sure
he understood what his guest just said
when he asked the specialist to explain it all again.

I was not sure how the man would make his point again
so with thousands, possibly tens-of-thousands
invisibly listening
along with me—we all leaned in, like silence itself
to the radio voice who then told us all about the brain's
plasticity—he had doubted it himself, he said—
for many years, decades, really; he'd heard a colleague

assert the theory thirty years or so before. "A crank"
who he knew now had been a visionary all along
and led him to the realization
that he'd been wrong about all he'd known about
the brain. Being able to see beyond one's earlier position, that
point-of-view, was the key that freed him
to reject each former hypothesis that he'd maintained.

This was the brain, at any age—making new connections.
And to abandon old neural connections for new
pathways seemed the very
hallmark of consciousness and our humanity.
But how many of us ever really see past a prior understanding?
And abandon it completely? This man
of science moved me most when he finally admitted

how wrong he'd been—in every other hypothesis
he'd made. Moving unknowingly from error
to error, without a sense of
progress is what made him become himself—
even if all our work seems like nothing but the sum of all our errors—
it will have been good to share our work, nevertheless.

FAMILY SECRETS

Out of the cauldrons in each fireplace of childhood,
some boil into view, roused from the flames
of their own making, they seep, these fragments

from shredded letters and conversations heard
partially when the kids are finally asleep and parents
and other relatives believe they can finally speak

freely of who did what to whom, how, and when,
and all the lurid details of the various devastations—
the raised voices rising to the highest rooms

where the children lie wide awake and listening,
as I was when I first heard our elders speak of it:
the story of the first American generation's

undoing; the one who married the neighborhood
bully, who used to give us what I thought were
clown ties, the aunt who never had kids but

may have had a daughter, the woman you thought
was also your aunt, her youngest sister; and the story
worsens when questions of the daughter's father arise.

So, when you're finally ready to ask the one person
alive who may know the whole story, and you ask,
you can almost hear the covered wagons of generations

circling in her voice, as if she's been waiting for you
to ask, and the closest you'll ever come to a revelation
of what you and your cousins will always now suspect

are the last words your mother will ever say to you
on the subject: "Oh, but that was years ago! What
does it matter now? What difference would knowing

the truth now really make?" And you know deep down
your mother's right. Nevertheless, you still fear the man's
wickedness is still there, inside you, in your blood. It is

of course inside you but also it is there with the righteous
anger of all the women who live inside you, too, their
argument is right there in your heart, still ticking in your pulse.

And they lived through it, and they took the secret of that
travesty to their graves. And in your blood you can hear
them saying, oh, they are saying, you'll live with it, too!

THE INVISIBLE THREAD

As to who is to be believed, and who is not to be believed, you can trust no one.
    —Vladimir Putin, Helsinki Summit, July 2018

As to who is to be believed, now you tell me.
Once I asked a Holocaust survivor if he
ever altered the facts to a published story.
And if so, why. "Yes. But it must be our secret!"

But now that everyone is gone—all who may
be harmed in knowing, even the story's teller,
what if I were to tell you the whole scene?:
Our storyteller, arrested in the Warsaw Ghetto

Uprising, was led to a cattle car (at Umshlagplatz
heading to Treblinka, then only a death-camp)
with his fiancé, Fredzia, Freesia—like the flower—

consoling her, or trying to, when his eyes met
his uncle's. Then those of his uncle's mistress.
Who could blame him for leaving this detail out?

I know of no other details he left out.
But other rewritings really did give me pause
and made me question all prior conversations.
Two stories: both concerning his parents.

Specifically, how they died: His mother, Sabina,
who'd played Carmen for Warsaw's Opera
(a photo he received after the war confirmed it)
died when "a stray bomb (in the Nazi Invasion

of Warsaw) struck the building where she received
treatment for ovarian cancer." The cancer part—
that's true! His father, Henryk, Chief Surgeon

of Warsaw's Jewish Hospital, he told me was shot:
"gunned down by an SS in the Warsaw Ghetto."
He died in the Warsaw Ghetto. That, too, is true!

What proved to be true, in each account,
was something I learned later: His mother
Sabina had died of ovarian cancer. But a year
before the war began. And his father, Henryk,

did die in the Warsaw Ghetto. But not
from a gunshot. I had to go to Poland,
to Warsaw's Jewish Historical Institute,
to learn the whole story. We arrived at noon,

as the lights were turning off, one by one.
Closing early? That's when Basia poked in
and said something to a man sweeping, then

the lights turn on again. "No time to explain!"
Basia said. Then, we're led to another room,
where so many scoured the shelves like angels.

And in their pigeon-like movements, gradually
the archivists pulled down books, one: Notable
Pre-War Jewish Physicians, and in the dark photos
I recognized the survivor's doctor-father.

And in other photos, I also saw Henryk.
Then one archivist unearthed a document:
("Fire-blackened edges," he said, "But legible!")
It was Henryk's death certificate.

Then the archivist, now smiling, started speaking
in lavish, luscious syllables to Basia, who giggled.
Then turned to me so she could translate.

"He says your friend's father died of 'a karbunkle'
—from a wound he sustained while performing
emergency surgery in the Ghetto. From his own knife!"

Now I knew: his father died from his own knife.
Back in Ohio, the pink full moon of ceiling light
in the old man's kitchen flickered above us as I
asked him to translate his father's death certificate.

He says what I heard in Warsaw. But goes farther:
Adding that his father was forced to perform
an appendectomy with inadequate anesthesia.
Poor surgical tools. Unsanitary conditions.

No antibiotics to treat his father's wound.
So, what could have been easily cured,
even in that dark time, became lethal.

I forced myself to ask my next question.
"Why did you say before that he was shot?"
"They said it would make a better story!"

"Who said it would make a better story?"
"The editor," he said, who first published his book
in a small edition—at St. Ottilien (a monastery
converted to a DP camp—outside Dachau).

The book he wrote after waking from a coma.
Written in six months. The book he wrote
to "stab back at the shadows enveloping him"
that "threatened to rob him—of his sanity!"

Think of him "stabbing back at the shadows"
—his last name, which in German means
"staff of wood"—and shares a Teutonic root

with the word for the prison bars that surround
the panther in Rilke's poem: a creature so bone-
weary in his cage, he "no longer sees the world."

When one can no longer see the world,
so imprisoned in the mind, one might
make even one's prison a means of escape.
How can "the curtain in the mind" be raised?

And what is it that trembles, however briefly,
over the beast, surging like a wave across
the ripping ligature of his crouching frame?
For Rilke's panther, the answer's "an image"—

one that "plunges into the heart and is gone."
I thought then that maybe the good doctor
needed his parents' deaths to match his grief

in its intensity: those images, then, that he made
to numb his heart like taps of a morphine drip
given one too far along in illness to be cured.

But was his story too corrupted to be redeemed?
It would have been, I thought, if his book (in English)
had been marred by these two factual errors.
But it wasn't. (Whether they poisoned the first

edition, in Polish, I still don't know.) I could
breathe easier. For now. At least somewhat.
The lie was not in his book. Only in me, did
that restless serpent trouble the mirrored waters

of reflection. The eel in the proverbial ointment.
It surfaces now. Another thread nosedives—
into invisibility. Remember, if it pleases you, those

whom I have loved into being, with the man himself.
(Rest now, all—and you, old friend!) —As to who's
to be believed, and who is not, now you tell me.

MY BROTHER, THE POET, AT NINETEEN

If you were to ask him yourself, he'd say
Nothing probably, but anyone who knows him
Would tell you—once they knew you were alone—
That my brother is the poet, the poet they know.
Sure, he slings drinks for them all night
At the bar where he's their favorite bartender
(Even three decades later). The older couples bring him
Homemade treats, tickets to ballgames—the best seats.
And it's not that he goes out of his way to
Befriend the regulars, it's just that they have
(As some have explained) all fallen for him.
Maybe it's the way he listens to them
Cry into their drinks, and how he laughs with them
At God and the wrong world. He listens
Like a nurse dispensing reliable cures
With a smile and just enough bedside manner
To show the depths of his genius for empathy.
But that's not even the half of it.
They love him because they've come to know
Him, end of story. But as his brother
There are things I can add, too, beyond the ways
He's taught me to listen and see the world with him.
Like one time, when I helped him to bed,
After getting him drunk on his nineteenth birthday,
(Don't worry: it was legal then!) and when I turned
To leave, he asked me something, and I saw he was
Weeping, and when I asked him what's wrong, he said,
"Would we even know each other
If we weren't brothers?"

SIGHTINGS

What's the most unforgettable experience
you've had among the creaturely? I keep

circling back to a beach in St. Augustine.
Sunset. A light of halved peaches saturating

everything. Walking the shoreline with my
first wife, no sense of anything but our joy.

When maybe twenty feet off shore, my eyes
focus on a dorsal fin. I hear the two-note

theme from Jaws. But then another surfaces—
a smaller dorsal fin. And, for a time, we move

it seems as one organism, the white water
wrinkling, webbing the edges of our worlds.

Who knows how far we traveled together.
Or if anything like language passed between us.

But such magnetism! The larger dolphin
even seemed to bow, before they swam away.

"CITY DUCKS"

in fond memory of Richard Howard (October 13 1929—March 31 2022)

Sometimes what it takes for us to see what's already right in front of us
    and all the time is a man with an almost greasepaint moustache
        reminiscent of Groucho Marx
            but as if it had melted in the July heat
                as its bearer sits on a park bench in Washington Square Park
                    covered completely in pigeons
              or "city ducks" as my Art History Librarian baby sister
                  calls them mere days before on her
              accidental visit to Manhattan before I could show her
                the man who looked like a retired clown or a lost vaudeville comic
            whose former life has ended, so, rather than immolate himself in protest
                    he simply shakes his head
under a brown bag full of birdseed until he's emptied it completely on himself.
    And it is truly something to behold almost too much to see completely
        for you must watch the various
                children and parents stopping in their tracks
            to unpack, if ever, the visual enigma breathing before them
                    now and all of us.

Like a pilot light turned down to a faint blue flickering
    it seemed the man had turned
something inside himself to an egg-shell blue oblivion
    that was visible now only in the well-oiled machinery of birds
    who were made a more alluring and entrancing blue than fire could ever be
    at least here in the park today
where free-wheeling ranters and shirtless skateboarders in hair buns and beards
    were circling some invisible center holding all of us together
their movements and those
    of the unmoving man with clouds of gray Bozo hair
    as the relentless pigeons became the living emblems of his white garment
    as they stood on his shoulders, beer paunch,
    however briefly fluttering their wings and walking
    off mid-air into late afternoon
while we waited for our friend to arrive at any moment
    and I could barely contain my gratitude and happiness
for the strange man, still as any public statuary, who sat there now as if any one of
    our blue lives depended upon it.

ACKNOWLEDGMENTS

Many thanks to the editors of the following literary journals who published (or are soon to publish) the following poems, some in earlier versions:

American Literary Review: "My Brother, the Poet, at Nineteen" & "In The Book of Spells"

Connotations Press: An Online Artifact: "Seven for the Last Words of X"

Five Points: "Mission Statement," "Song for the Vultures," & "The Perplexities of Time and Space at Last Explained (Eventually, Despite Rain Delays)"

The Kenyon Review: "To Misunderstanding"

Literary Imagination: "The Invisible Thread"

Ploughshares: "To the Language Spoken in the County of Urgency"

Plume Poetry: "My Polish" & "Another Poem That I Can't Show to My Sweetheart's Parents"

Stronger Than Fear (Cave Moon Press): "To Misunderstanding"

"For the Language Spoken in the Country of Urgency" was translated into Italian by Alessandra Natale and read (in English and Italian) at the 2014 *Festival Internazionale di Poesia* (International Poetry Festival) in Genoa and Bogliasco, Italy (June, 2014); it was also nominated for a Pushcart Prize.

"Seven for the Last Words of X" was originally commissioned by Dean Whiteside, conductor of the Nashville Sinfonietta, to be read at a performance of Haydn's "The Seven Last Utterances of Christ On the Cross" (written in 1785) and was performed at Ingram Hall, Blair School of Music: Saturday, August 31, 2013 at 8 p.m. All proceeds went to the Shade Tree Free Clinic, Nashville, TN.

Special thanks to everyone at Vanderbilt University, especially to the English Department and Chair Dana Nelson and to the MFA Program and Director Major Jackson, and to Emily Hobbs and Rachel Mace; to VU, also abiding thanks for multiple Poindexter Endowment grants and sabbaticals that helped me complete this collection. And to Michael and Nic Knight, Mitch Austin, and Marcos Chavez of the Helene Wurlitzer Foundation in Taos, NM for wonderful conversations and lengthy stays in which many of these poems were written. Thanks to John Gosslee and Andrew Ibis and everyone at C & R Press for selecting this manuscript as the winner of the 2020 Winter Soup Bowl Chapbook competition and making the process so effortless. And special shout-outs to the following friends, mentors, family/fellow-travelers for crucial support & sustenance: Kate Daniels, Mark Jarman, Major & Didi Jackson, Sandy Solomon, Tony Earley, Lorrie Moore, Nancy Reisman, Georgia Court & Robin Radin, Peter Hooten, Draper Shreeve & Christopher Bram, Bhisham Bherwani, Stephen Massimilla, Frank Avella & Henry Van Kooy, Dave King & Frank Tartaglione, Christie Grotheim & Niklas Andersson, Abigail Redman & Andrew Holm-Hansen, Clisby Hall & Robert Zarabi, Martie Koehl, Natasha Caldwell, Glenn Kurtz, Gregory Mertl, Laren McClung, Jeff, Allison, Rowan, Amelia, Austin & Elliott Norton, Alfred Corn, Grace Schulman, Richard Howard, Edward Hirsch, (Jean Valentine & Lucie Brock-Broido, i.m.), and to more recent friends who have invigorated & sustained me: Duane DeRaad, Linda Naranjo & Scott Huebl (& the whole Los Gatos Friday "happy hour" gang), Lise Goett, Dora E. McQuaid, Pattie Traynor, Zhenevere Sophia Dao, Lex Williford, Ayden Graham, Claudia Tremblay, Christina de Gennaro, Eeva Siivonen, Natalie Voelker, Alexander Lumans, Eric Guinivan, Samyak Shertok.

My Mom & Dad. My Brother Ross & My Sister Stefanie.

And to Stephanie Elizondo Griest—for so much more than I can say!

C&R PRESS CHAPBOOKS

C&R Press hosts two chapbook selection periods from June to September and November to March each year. The Winter Soup Bowl and Summer Tide Pool Chapbook Series are open to new and established writers in poetry, fiction, essay and other creative writing.

2020 Winter Soup Bowl
My Roberto Clemente by Rick Hilles

2019 Summer Tide Pool
Inside the Orb of an Oracle by Dannie Ruth

2019 Winter Soup Bowl
The Magical Negro Reveals His Secret by Gabriel Green

2018 Summer Tide Pool
Yell by Sarah Sousa

2018 Winter Soup Bowl
Paleotemptestology by Bertha Crombet
White Boys from Hell by Jeffrey Skinner

2017 Summer Tide Pool
Atypical Cells of Undetermined Significance by Brenna Womer

2017 Winter Soup Bowl
Heredity and Other Inventions by Sharona Muir
On Inaccuracy by Joe Manning

2016 Summer Tide Pool
Cuntstruck by Kate Northrop
Relief Map by Erin M. Bertram
Love Undefined by Jonathan Katz

2016 Winter Soup Bowl
Notes from the Negro Side of the Moon by Earl Braggs
A Hunger Called Music: A Verse History in Black Music by Meredith Nnoka

www.ingramcontent.com/pod-product-compliance
Lightning Source LLC
Chambersburg PA
CBHW051703040426
42446CB00009B/1277